"Inner Whispers"

Messages From

A Spirit Guide

Volume III

"Inner Whispers"
Messages From A Spirit Guide (Volume III)

Title: *"Inner Whispers"*
Messages From Spirit Guides:
Volume III

Author: April Crawford

Publisher: Connecting Wave
2629 Foothill Blvd.
Unit # 353
La Crescenta, CA 91214
www.ConnectingWave.com

ISBN: 978-0-9823269-4-7

For Author Information:
www.AprilCrawford.com

Other books via April Crawford:
www.AprilCrawfordBooks.com

Book Design: Allen Crawford

For Permissions: Publisher@ConnectingWave.com

NOTE: Since this is Volume III of these messages, the contents listings continue from Volume II. Accordingly, the next numbered message in this Volume III starts with message number 105.

CONTENTS

CONTENTS

CONTENTS

CONTENTS

***

Forward by VERONICA

"We continue our commitment to the expansion of your soul.

Know that the whispers are within you, as well as in the pages of this book.

There is an eternal perspective that will always seek the presence of your energy. Never doubt the willingness of spirit to reach out, whether needed or not.

Trust yourself.

Your journey continues toward the connection with your soul.

Our hope is that the linear words on these pages will bring comfort to all."

-VERONICA

About April Crawford

April Crawford is a natural Full Body Open Deep Trance Channel and Spirit Medium. These are relatively rare.

Because April is able to be completely open and without any fear of the process whatsoever, the nonphysical entities and guides who come through are able to <u>totally</u> integrate with the physical, while at the same time not blending at all with April's personality. They therefore have <u>full</u> physical and emotional, control during their "visits".

This allows zero distortion or "coloring" by April, and also allows them to walk around the room, go out for a walk in the night air, keep their eyes wide open when they speak, and even eat or drink if they wish (but most choose not to).

These physical abilities are one of the things that allow VERONICA… the name we have given to the highly evolved nonphysical entity and guide that gave us all of the messages in this book… to give readings and have long, fully interactive conversations over a speakerphone, and even to write in longhand herself (not automatic writing), or type on a computer keyboard, and even use a computer mouse or computer touch screen.

You can see videos of VERONICA speaking while April Crawford is in deep trance at:

www.AprilCrawford.com

April routinely allows many different entities and aspects of entities to come through, and they have a full range of motion and emotion. Some who are in-between physical lives, for example, have cried uncontrollably or expressed total joy when we advised them of certain things about their physical lives. But the messages in this book are all from VERONICA.

About VERONICA

The Spirit Guide that wrote all of these messages is VERONICA.

"VERONICA", as we call "her", is an evolved nonphysical entity and guide. "She" refers to herself as a nonphysical consciousness and she leans toward female energy when we consult with her, even though VERONICA has been both sexes and she has told me her favorite physical life was as a male in Bristol England.

VERONICA has enjoyed physical incarnation and has done so many times. This experience helps her in her consultations with those currently incarnated. Of course this is in addition to her ability to "read" the energy of any person, place, or thing, in addition to her many (very many) associates on the "other side" at all levels of evolution and expertise.

(Note: Some other entities and individuals in-between physical lives that come through April Crawford express themselves as male energies, so it is not because April is female that VERONICA expresses herself as female.)

You may wonder about VERONICA's name. Actually, it is a name we gave her many years ago. When she first came through, it was rather amazing and rather dramatic (and VERONIA was not the first to come through, but was certainly the most intense). At that time, "she" did not give us a name when we asked, saying basically that "Labels are not necessary". She went on to say that if we needed a label, that we could choose whatever name we wanted.

We chose the name "VERONICA", and it stuck. Now, even other nonphysical beings who visit via April Crawford's Open Deep Trance Channeling know exactly who VERONICA is if we mention her. It seems that things get around in the cosmos rather quickly, and rather completely!

All of VERONICA's messages are either spoken or written by her in first, final, and only draft. There is never any editing of a single sentence or word. As facilitator, I (Allen) do sometimes arbitrarily add some punctuation, usually commas. Also, VERONICA never uses the word "and" when writing, instead always choosing the "+" or "&" symbols. I usually change these to the word "and".

-Allen, Facilitator for April Crawford

105

The Harmony Of The Soul

"The harmony of the soul often eludes those in the linear. Interaction with other energies can incite a battle of wits that can preclude the necessary alignment with one's own vibration.

When a soul incarnates within its soul group, there are often continuing dramas that thread themselves through many lives. A particular imbalance between two energies may take several lifetimes to emerge into a more tranquil interaction.

If you find yourself in a web of discomfort, it is important to remember that it is but a chapter in the evolvement that is being created between you. The dance will continue until it is resolved. The despair of this participation interaction may be alleviated in the next life.

In the case of the current interaction, the snares from past moments can lay in one's path as the life proceeds in the now. Often two souls of great connection participate at this level.

If one is able to look at it from this perspective, it is possible to understand where the difficulty originated and where it is going.

Know that you participate on many levels and that not all of them are difficult.

Stay the course, for in the eternal crescendo all will be resolved. You will find the place and tranquility you seek.

Be strong."

-VERONICA

106

Forgiveness... Is It Possible?

"The soul learns much through the pathways of physical existence. The dramas created leaving one to ponder the ability to put oneself into a scenario and perceive from another's viewpoint.

Many wrongs are endured by those who trusted another... injury to the heart a constant reminder that some energies blindly push their way through a life with little or no care to those they bruise.

What of those who are injured? Are they required to bear the scars of cruelty endlessly? In some viewpoints it seems so, however, it is important to remember that forgiveness is often the pathway to liberation from one who would cause injury. By taking their power away through non-engagement in the negative exchange, one <u>can</u> achieve separation.

The next step to strengthen the resolve is letting go of the pain by releasing the feelings attached to the exchange.

Not an easy task, however, a necessary one if you are desiring to release yourself totally. To continue without forgiveness only beckons more in future moments. Often it becomes a pattern resulting in a repetitive moment.

It is important to realize that some who would injure you do not realize what they are doing. They participate in an unconscious moment triggered by their own pain.

Decide within yourself that it is possible to forgive. Venture down the path and release the negativity. It will not immediately fix everything, but it will put you in a greater creative arena.

Forgive and release.

Further participation may not be possible with them.

Forgive and release.

Make your way to freedom & peace.

Forgive."

-VERONICA

107

Balance in the Present

"Becoming physical is indeed a great undertaking. The benefits are many if one can navigate a steady path towards the evolving of the soul.

It is often that we are asked about the future. Many in their belief systems feel that the future is a pre-written script that if followed, will take them to the next level.

The fascination of what the future will bring negates the power of the present. The present is really the only place where one can create their future moment.

It is imperative to stay calm and focused now. Each choice made is another facet of what will come. It can not be predicted, only created.

That creative moment is your present. By staying balanced without the hindrance of fear, there is more clarity to have the life you desire.

Reaching deep within to maintain the balance is the key. Separating from all the chaos to that quiet place within will help.

The balance maintained will aid you in your path to clarity. It is, however, in the now not the future.

One cannot have a flower without first planting the seeds and enriching the earth beneath.

Stay focused.

Be quiet.

Balance in the now will create your future, which will then become your next now. As you can see, it is really an eternal present moment.

Be powerful.

Be balanced."

--VERONICA

108

Self Doubt

"When aspiring to create and manifest in the linear, it is important to consider your energy input. Often the difficulty of bringing manifestations into the linear is interfered upon by the exact one who is trying to bring them in.

How you think about yourself and your abilities becomes clear when things either go well or do not.

Examine your opinions and personal energy often. In truthfulness see how those moments have an effect upon your experience. You are connected to your soul, which feels powerful in the moment, however, your self-doubt can often derail the best laid plans.

It's not easy to examine the self. Earlier experience, which includes childhood and past lives, can aid the self into feeling powerless and victimized.

Whenever possible, attempt to see a moment clearly without the opinions interfering.

Pure thought is the best approach.

We realize it would be easier to blame outside forces for derailments, however, the courage to examine the self would be the best route.

Stay still.

Look doubt in the eye and see it for what it is.

Be more powerful and self assured, your soul is.

Eliminate the doubt and embrace your power. It's really the only way."

--VERONICA

109

Emotional Healing

"Many who incarnate into the physical find themselves at some point battling a disease of the body. It may appear to be rooted in genetics or the environment. However, perhaps the real inception lies in emotional turmoil that may need healing. This could be a moment from the current lifetime as well as a past life.

As one walks through the life, it is important to listen to your emotions, not just to act and react with them. An understanding of the effect that energy has on your body supersedes many ideas your culture may have upon health.

We would recommend awareness of your emotional strengths and weaknesses. If you indeed find yourself lacking, then appropriate attention to healing would be in order.

Spend moments energetically transmitting the power of your soul. Look at the situation honestly even if at first you find it difficult.

By removing negative emotion while offering healing, the probability of disease free participation could exist.

It is not easy being a participant on the earth. Your best defense is to address yourself emotionally, whenever possible. Yes, eventually the body will pass from the earth plane, however, the journey does not have to be emotionally or physically painful.

Call upon spirit to assist. Return to the core of your energy for support. Heal difficult emotion immediately. The mistake of not addressing it will result in difficulty at some point.

Feel the emotion within.

Offer it solace when needed.

Return to the soul to support and heal the negative emotions.

Emotionally healing...the best soul–made, homemade, remedy you can give yourself."

--VERONICA

110

The Journey With Your Soul

"As one walks through a life, it is sometimes difficult to feel the full connection with the soulful energy. If it is indeed a journey, how then does one make that journey with the soul?

It is important to remember that by incarnating, one establishes a singularity. In the body with all of the linear distractions, that separateness can create a vivid loneliness.

Finding oneself in the physical environment without the companionship of the soul can be daunting, even for the most advanced energy.

Take a moment to separate from all the chaos of the day. Remember the peaceful vibration from which you came.

Allow that energy to fill your thoughts. By re-investigating that relationship within you there will be better opportunity to know yourself. The ability to reconnect will guide you through the most difficult of times.

Allow the soul to walk with you through this life. It deserves the connection as much as you miss it.

Reconnect.

Walk the path together.

This life need not be separate from your soul's energy."

--VERONICA

111

Walking A New Path

"Many times we have encountered those in the linear who are tired of walking down familiar paths. They are often ones where the outcome is predictable and the energy ever devolving into greater negativity.

Physical life is full of opportunity to change direction. One has to be full of courage to do so. A belief system in your ability to choose is also needed.

Whatever has occurred, you do have the ability to change it. All of the drama surrounding the change may appear to be difficult, but only if you enable it to do so. The confusion arises when allowing inappropriate drama to continue. It begins to feel very commonplace. Those in that energy space usually feel unable to change their course.

Spirit will assist you in your quest to walk a new path. Feeling like a victim of circumstance only enables the negativity to stay.

Choose to change direction.

At first it may feel awkward or lonely. However, put one foot in front of the other as you walk the new path.

Your soul will accompany you on the journey.

A new path is a new life which brings the probability of happiness and connection.

Take the first step."

--VERONICA

112

The Strength To Change It

"In the physical realm it becomes easy to allow negative energy to persuade you that you are not worthy.

This self-deprecating despair overwhelms many who are living a difficult life. In an attempt to correct this, one may often look at it through their physical eyes. In doing so they become overwhelmed, thus powerless to do anything about it.

This 'stuck feeling' is a huge concern for those participating in the linear. One needs to reach deep into the soul to find the strength to change it. Perhaps the view from one's physical eyes is not the one to dwell on.

The spiritual eyes of the soul offer a perspective that is unconditional and forgiving. Looking at the situation from the eternal can bring hope to what seems unsolvable. When the physical energy has dwindled, the soul can help you dig down to a new level of courage. No matter how dire the drama, the soulful energy can transform you to a new level of understanding.

When faced with turmoil, let your soul comfort you. Look out onto your world with spiritual eyes for a new perspective and solution.

The soul is tireless in its pursuit of your well being."

--VERONICA

113

The Garden of Life

"The choice to incarnate is never a standard one. Each soul makes the leap into physical for different reasons. There are some who enjoy the process and grow with each event. Others do not incarnate often and find the whole process too separate and tedious to gather evolution from. Regardless of the various levels of perception, each of you tend the garden of your life specifically.

It is important to plant seeds of experience, trim the leaves as the seedling begins to sprout, water and pay attention to all the variables that will help your flowers grow.

Along the way it is sometimes necessary to weed the garden so as not to distract from the magnificence of it.

Yes, weeds can be a negative participation but the importance of your focus upon the flower supersedes the weeds. It is your responsibility to remove the negativity so that all may blossom and grow.

Not becoming attached to the destruction that the weeds represent is a very important one. Reach deep into your energy, tend your garden. Spring is always just around the corner in your heart and soul.

Take advantage of the sunshine and realize that rainy days are equally valuable.

In the end it will be the flowers that you will remember, and the joy their fragrance gives you."

--VERONICA

114

Fearless

"In the current reality it may appear that it is at the brink of disaster. Every moment being filled with a crescendo of negativity. One wonders where it will all lead to as the parameters of your world wavers. Many of you feel that the end is near, but is it?

Without fear, it is a beginning.

Know that spirit is ever present for all within every heart beat in the physical. Often in the chaos, one feels separated from their soul while walking through their lives. It is important to remember that you create your reality and it must be done from a fearless place.

Being physical at this time does require great courage. So much fear is being hurled into the mass consciousness that many of you have become paralyzed within it.

Attempt to regain your balance while moving past fear into your own soul. It is in this space you will find the bravery to defeat negativity.

By creating in a fearless space, there is great hope for your planet. Connecting with others positively will change the imbalance that is now occurring.

The end is not near. What will happen is the evolution of the planet and the advancement of your soul.

Be fearless."

--VERONICA

115

Seek Your Soul

"Often in the physical, it is difficult to determine if one is evolving spiritually. Dramas unfold causing great confusion in the hearts of those incarnate.

In pursuit of the truth, outside linear input can often mislead those who seek a plateau of spiritual connection. It is spirit, and only spirit, in harmony with you that will lead to the advancement of your soul.

It is important to take time in the chaos of a life to center one's perception of the self. A quiet thought has great worth when seeking spiritual alignment.

If you find yourself in a sea of doubt or a confused arena of perspective, seek your soul. As we have said many times, it will not abandon you... ever.

Physical life offers opportunity to experience, but the imperfect energy can often derail your progress. Your spiritual perspective can repair the misalignment. All one need do is step back from the dramas and align with spirit.

Feel the pulse of yourself and the pulse /vibration of your soul. It will make a difference. This life is but one chapter in a novel of your evolvement. It will resolve itself if you reach out spiritually.

Go ahead.

Give it a try."

-VERONICA

116

Power of One

"In the current culture much is made of all the negativity. Enactments of hate, lies, and unbalance are fairly the standard moment in most environments.

If you find yourself surrounded in a negative place, it is important to seek balance within yourself.

We realize that most of you do not know where to begin to create that moment. It all starts within this clarity of balance that will create a positive harmony. Being constantly bombarded with darkness, it may seem impossible to find the light of day.

Each breath that you take can be another step towards joy. Of course outside influences are difficult to ignore but the alternative is dire to the core of your soul.

Each day face the negative with the assurance of the joy of your soul. If it is buried then dig deeply to find it. Do not allow the dark energy to defeat your perspective.

Some of you are fairly entrenched in the negativity around you. Reverse that process by finding one thing to be joyful about. You might not have to dig as deeply as you think.

Separate from all the propaganda seeded with fear. It will feed upon itself until it overcomes you.

Knowingly set it aside. Find the positive in the sea of darkness. Refuse to join the negative grouping of energy.

The power of your own energy will aid you. Spirit will extend its love in your direction. Say no to fear and negativity. Participate from a bright perspective. It is your only defense in this global moment.

Balance is attainable.

Refuse to be one of the masses.

Be singular and joyful.

It can and will change the world..... one person at a time.

The power of one is more than is known."

--VERONICA

117

Rough Times In The Linear

"In the linear the feeling of separation is often expanded as one feels his or her way through the sea of chaos. Most feel the void and become fearful that their connection with their soul may be forever out of their reach.

It is important to realize that those in spirit are always moving past any impediments to connecting with those they love in the linear.

Close your eyes when fearful and feel the touch of spirit. The warmth of that embrace can supersede any detachment one may feel while in the physical form.

Spirit senses when the disconnect occurs, and moves forcefully to reconnect. Allow the energy to proceed. We realize it may be difficult, but open yourself to the probability if at all possible.

We have stated before that spirit will never abandon you. This remains the most stable connection in the linear world as spirit moves forward to connect.

Always know that these moments of warmth and love continue. Pay attention in times of trouble so that the connection may become more stable.

It is the best possible moment when the soul can smooth the rough edges of a linear moment. It is not your imagination, the work of spirit is profound. Believe in the moment and all will be well.

The soul has the power to smooth out all of the roughness. One simply needs to allow for that to occur.

Close your eyes and believe.

Relief will be forthcoming."

                                    --VERONICA

118

Giving and Receiving Energy

"We are aware of your season of giving [December].

It relates to many cultures that have existed upon your earth plane. From our perspective, the moment should be expanded beyond the boundaries that have been put in place by time.

It is also important in the giving to allow for the receiving of energy to be in place. It is a moment of respect for the self to receive others who wish to give to you.

Everything in your universe is based on give and take of energy. This concept goes right down to the atoms and molecules that create the reality you all exist within.

Remember to open your energy to the concept of receiving. It is impossible in the linear to continue giving energy without the possibility of receiving. So enjoy the moment of emphasis and continue to create.

The universe in its solidarity is counting upon the exchange.

Be kind to others and yourself.

It is the only way."

--VERONICA

119

Focus

"Being physical in this particular time frame offers many challenges to energies attempting to maneuver through it. Those who are more experienced feel the lack of supportive energy from the environment. Younger souls find the journey almost impossible, with the many manifestations of drama and difficulties.

With such constricting energy, it is important for all on the physical plane to be creative and maintain clear focus.

It can be the goal, the idea, or the representation, but be sure to be focused clearly upon whatever it is you wish to create.

The availability of distraction at this time is abundant. Be very sure of where your attention lies. If one focuses on a mishap or difficulty it is incredibly easy to create more.

Stay the course no matter what outside forces assail your life. Keep your eye on the center of the target.

It is a difficult time, but the ability to rise above and beyond it is available. Maintain your focus. You will be successful. Stay the course."

-VERONICA

120

Be In The Flow

"In times of trouble, most tighten their energy in defense. It is a natural reaction when the vibration does not match your own.

Everything in reality has an ebb and flow of energy. It is the core of all physical manifestations. It is important to keep the self relaxed and participating in a healthy vibration.

We realize that by closing off the soul one may feel momentarily protected. However, in the long run the ultimate participation comes from an ebb and flow. Keeping closed does not allow for the natural progression of the soul.

We would suggest when events are difficult, to maintain the free flow vibration of the soul as it comes through. In the physical it is sometimes not easy. The soul on the other hand, will rise to the occasion if given access to do so.

We say when dealing with trying situations, allow the soul to participate. Keep the linear in line with the soul.

By creating a free flow of energy you are designing a vortex of vibration that is your own. It is the most secure way to move past the difficulty.

Keep the ebb and flow of your soul at the forefront of your thoughts. Never allow it to stand still. Your vibration is who you really are.

Be in the flow.

Once you are comfortable, allow it to take you beyond the moment. Suddenly the way may clear, offering more opportunity for evolvement.

Stay calm.

Stay focused.

Be in the flow."

--VERONICA

121

Imperative to the Spiritual Connection

"In the physical experience there are often times when its thickness of the energy becomes unbearable. No matter which way one turns, a dead end of impasse greets them.

Many become tired by the pressure needed to push through. Giving up becomes a standard choice at each apparent dead end.

A sense of great loneliness appears, as one who tries to get through struggles against the difficult energy.

It takes a lot of focus to live at this time in the linear. We caution that during such intensity it is also prudent to allow spirit to engage you as well. It may feel awkward to focus and release seemingly at the same time, however, it an attainable endeavor.

From a spiritual perspective the flow of energy needs to maintain fluidity to have the proper impact. It is important to focus, but the allowance of the energy flow is imperative to the spiritual connection.

We realize we repeat often the need for the spiritual relationship. It will be repeated until all find their place in the soulful connection moment. Sometimes, consistency of loving statements are required when one is faced with difficulty in the linear.

Spirit reaches towards you at all times. Allow yourself to reach back, <u>while</u> thoughtfully focusing in your life.

At the end of the experience it will be the connecting moments that are most vivid in memory."

--VERONICA

122

Past Life Energy

"In your current life experience there can often be incidents of unrest and difficulty that appear to have no connections to your current moment. It is, however, somewhat impossible to dismiss the negative energy as it impacts the now moment.

All of you have had lives where the energy created remains unresolved. Some of these lives manifested negative moments that had no opportunity in a physical enactment to resolve themselves.

The life ended, taking with it this energy wishing to be concluded. In some cases there is a huge build up of this energy from concurrent and parallel lives.

Those who find themselves in this type of moment are often confused with the influence those lives have upon their current ones. More confusion arises when the inability to get "anything right in the moment" reflects upon the life they are living now.

It is important to consider the energy of a past life, while attempting to work through present dramas. Being able to separate the past from the now is valuable.

Consider the multiple aspects of your physical experience. It may enable you to maintain your power and progress in this one."

--VERONICA

[Note from Allen: While it may seem as if "past life" information is not readily available, there are many practitioners of "Past Life" Regression practicing worldwide. Other intuitives can also help you gain insight into "Past Life" issues. For nonphysical entities and guides such as VERONICA, these issues and past life threads are

as obvious as it would be to you looking at a friend and being able to see what color hair they have. In fact this is a considerable understatement since many people may color their hair but reincarnational threads and dramas cannot be so altered or disguised.]

:

123

Changing Patterns

"It is inevitable in the linear for one to create patterns of thoughts and behavior. Some are productive, while others hinder growth significantly.

When you were a child, drawing patterns was a way to increase your participation. There was always the need, however, to move on from a continuous pattern that was no longer interesting to create. If there was unconscious participation then one could continue the pattern endlessly. Once fully conscious, however, there was a desperate need to discontinue.

Awareness of monotonous patterns is essential to growth both in physical and spiritual. It is important each day to take a moment to look honestly at patterns you are currently creating. Without this self check, your patterns can become connected to others causing more complicated patterns to emerge in quite a dramatic display of negativity.

Many become overwhelmed while not truly understanding what has occurred. While quite impossible to change others, you can increase your awareness. Change your patterns and release yourself from difficult situations.

We advise an honest look at your patterns daily. Some are repeated endlessly while new ones emerge all the time. Often it's surprising that the root of a problem grew from your own patterns of behavior. By recognizing this you become more powerful in creating your reality. There will always be other participants, but by remaining aware of the probabilities of a pattern, you create an ability to be more in control.

We understand that many who read this will already feel victim to created negativity. Your biggest chance to change that comes directly from you. Change the pattern, change the reality.

Even the most subtle change will have an effect on the energy.

Take time to look at yourself honestly. Make the changes.

You are the creator of your reality. It is time to take back the ownership."

--VERONICA

124

The Decision To Be Here

"The physical environment is one of great density. To create the solid moments, great attention is paid to the intensity necessary to create it all.

It is often not a comfortable place for those with a finer vibration. Many feel out of place in such a wild territory such as physical. Wondering in fact, why they would make such a decision to be here at all.

In the eternal energy there are times where more evolved healing energies are called upon to be of service. Incarnating in a reality where their higher vibration can help balance the density is the primary reason.

It is a time of great movement in the linear, so there is an abundant amount of souls who have made the decision to be here.

Once in the form, however, there can be an occurrence of the dramatic that can cause complete memory to escape those who have volunteered. Knowing on some level they need to be here, but for what, remains a big question.

To find the answer, attempt to settle quietly into your energy. Block out the chitter chatter of the day and remember why.

Balancing energy in this environment is a big endeavor. There are a lot of energies like yourself that are awakening to their purpose.

Lending your ability to balance energy is a huge undertaking, but you would not have come here without the desire to do it.

Focus. Meditate. Be one with your soulful energy. It is what you came here for.

The physical reality will rebound positively with your endeavors. Yes. Your energy is important. Align. Send the healing. It is your purpose this time around."

--VERONICA

125

A Viewpoint of Your Life

"When one is incarnate, it is easy to become completely absorbed by the linear dramatic life. The focus is immediate and compacted, leaving the soul distracted by all the solidness and theatrics.

If one is to truly evolve, it is important to step outside of the life. A view of the bigger picture is often helpful when trying to determine your advancement.

Take in each day a moment where the energy is not one of the linear. A moment where a sense of oneness and tranquility overrides everything else. It does not have to be a standard meditation process. It can be as simple as a walk, listening to music, or appreciating the breeze upon your face as you sit in a favorite spot.

The idea of a private moment is often foreign to most of you. A breath of tranquility, no matter what the source, can give you a view point of your life.

Take a pause.

Separate from the little picture and participate with the bigger one. The one where your soul resides. It will make a difference. By putting the dramatics of the day that appear so enormous in a different perspective, you will be able to see clearly the direction to go.

Design your moment of meditation. It is certainly all right to do so.

Become one with the bigger picture. Your path may be easier in the linear because of it.

Take the pause.

Become clear."

--VERONICA

126

Why We Do This

"In our interaction with those in the physical, one of the main inquiries is the reason why we do this.

One would think, that once free of the linear, that an energy would desire to be in the open space of eternity. Why take on the burden of a thick energetic environment when it appears unnecessary?

The answer is that in essence we are all one. Each with individual experience and memories that remain while still being connected.

We are able to see the beauty and vibrance of your soulful energy so that we may remind you of its potential. It is very easy to become clouded in viewpoint while living a life. If our perspective can offer greater clarity so that you may evolve then we all evolve in harmony in our respective environments. The ripple of higher conscious moments reaches all energy at some level.

At our stage of advancement it is joyous to feel the raising of energy in a positive powerful way.

We reach out to all who live in the physical domain to remind you of your brilliance and of ability to create. There are no silly questions. We feel your desire to know and we respond without judgment.

Know that the love of spirit is endless. This is why we participate, so that all may have more clarity and knowing."

--VERONICA

127

Physical Reality is in Transition

"The linear is a canvas of expression that is created deep within the soul. At this time of existence much is said of the unstable energy that permeates everyone 's reality.

The greatest desire is to reach a place of peace and tranquility. The greatest need is for stability in and on all levels of physical participation. Most would settle for a good day of connection to their soul.

Yes the physical reality is in transition. What direction it takes is dependent upon the energy participation of each and every one of you.

The internal relationship to your own soul is the best path to take in this chaotic time-frame.

Participate simply. Be attentive to the whispers of your soul. Your involvement in this raising of consciousness is crucial.

You are not just a linear being victim to circumstance. You are an abundant soul having a linear experience. What you express outwardly from your soul does make a difference.

Create time with your soul. Practice random acts of kindness whenever possible. The pool of negativity is large but if each of you consciously decided not to refresh it, eventually it would diminish.

Fill your reality instead with positive action. You may feel ineffective at first, especially if you are surrounded by negativity.

Forge ahead hand in hand with your soulful energy. Express those moments of the canvas of your own life. Everything is connected.

Be the one drop of energy expression that changes everything.

It is possible."

-VERONICA

128

Hearing the Energy of Your Own Soul

"In the linear the voices of many create a wall of sound that can keep one from hearing the energy of their own souls.

It is important at these times to clear the mind of unwanted chitter chatter. A reflective moment can allow one to really be able to listen to their internal voice. If a standard meditation does not resonate with you, then consideration of alternatives is imperative.

Many may begin to reach that level of serenity by connecting with nature. A walk in the confines of a natural moment may be just the remedy required. Music is often another alternative to achieving the internal silence necessary.

It's a very dense reality that all are participating with at this time. The connection to your soul is the best avenue to tread. Realize that by striving to listen to the whispers of your soul there is hope for the now. By having your now in hand the future is that much easier to create.

It is better to create your reality in the serenity of your own thoughts than to endeavor to go amongst the noise and chaos of the current mass consciousness.

Do not follow the crowd.

Go within.

Listen.

Listen intently to your own thoughts.

Stay connected.

Decide to be centered.

Listen to the voice of your soul.

It's the only way."

                        --VERONICA

129

Loss of Pets

"The physical environment offers an intense participation of energy not felt anywhere else. Often the lightness of one's spirit becomes entangled in all of the drama, making one feel burdened and isolated.

The representation of energy in physical form has great impact upon others whether it is arriving or leaving. The ones left behind, so to speak, feel the absence of energy and respond to it often dramatically.

Enter the animal with its unique ability to remain unconditional in the worst of circumstances. Pets as well survive the end of physical life, move into spiritual arenas, and reincarnate.

Know that these experiences are valid and important just as those of the human nature. A dog or a cat are different vibrations of energy participation in their own evolution. Often they are more advanced than their human counterparts. The same animal may reincarnate repeatedly with the same human to assist in their ascension.

One only need to look deeply into a pet's eyes to know that this is true.

Be assured that reconnection is in place regardless of circumstance. You will participate again with them.

The connection is stronger, sometimes more profound, than a human one.

Animals lack the ability to be judgmental, selfish, or unloving. All of the drama is meaningless to them. It is only the connection with you that is meaningful.

They allow themselves to be tortured, abused, and rescued so that humans will get the lesson.

They will return.

Without doubt."

-VERONICA

130

The First Thing
That Should Be Addressed

"The energy of the planet at this time is chaotic in the best of circumstances. Each person participating can feel the frenetic energy as it emanates from the surface.

This energy can bring fear into the hearts of those who cannot assimilate it all properly.

What should one do in times of trouble?

The first thing that should be addressed is your own belief system. The ability to rise above the difficult energy is crucial. Know that you do have the power to balance all situations. Even if it is a mass consciousness moment, realize that every drop of positive thought projected into the most dire situation does help.

Secondly, having a sense of well being while appreciating your own skills of creativity. Not every experience is perfect. Sometimes even the difficult ones can garner much growth and perspective. Do not judge difficulty harshly. Realize that you are capable of contouring any experience. Allow yourself the lesson, even if it's not pleasant. Take from it the created new energy and use it to continue your evolution.

Nothing is lost.

Nothing is wasted.

Decide within yourself that you have value while learning the lesson.

Whenever possible allow this energy to be released into your reality. It helps with the planet, others, and yourself.

The time of ascending to a new level of perspective is at hand. Be the one who embraces all of it and grows.

If enough of you participate in this way, the transition will be easier for all.

The time is now."

-VERONICA

131

What Should I Do?

"In times of uncertain reality it is easy to become attached to negative outcomes. Normally the individual would keep their thoughts aligned, but with all the input of negativity, even the most stalwart mind can be at risk.

It is a time of reaching deep into the soul and remembering beyond the linear. If attachment to the timeline is the primary source of energy, there may be difficulty in creating one's reality.

A moment of courage is required when all the energy of the environment is in chaos. Realize that this is but one chapter in the story of you and your energy. No matter what occurs, the continuance of your soul is a fact.

Take the lessons of a harsh reality and put them to good use. Appreciate the small moments of success as they will attract more if encouraged to do so.

Love those whom you cherish with great warmth. Those playing in this drama have participated with you in other moments.

Attempt to clean up the small pockets of chaos as they approach you. It will help soothe the mass consciousness energy so that the whole environment may heal and evolve.

Maintain the fierceness of knowing who you are and the role you play in this environment. Know that you are far more than just the face you see in the mirror.

Keep counsel with the truth. The truth of your incarnation and that of your eternal soul.

Be a participant in this life not an observer. Create, expand, and grow, and make life happen. Do not let life happen to you.

You are the creator.

You have the possibility of changing it all.

Have courage and do it."

-VERONICA

132

Time

"When physical, the most complicated relationship seems to be with time. Its endless march towards oblivion fills all those incarnate with dread.

"The march against time."

"Is time on my side?"

"The lack of enough time."

All of these statements ring true for most in this linear experience.

There are a lot of anxious moments spent when considering time. It can leave the participant rather paralyzed when attempting to maneuver through the ups and downs of their experience.

We suggest that placing oneself outside of the timeline whenever possible. Attempt to create a timeless element in your experience. There really is not a standard length for time. It is perceived by each of you differently. So deciding upon what that is, and developing some control of your perceptions, time may not be the enemy that most of you are fighting.

Take some space everyday to consciously view time from an outside perspective. You are actually the creator of time.

Simply decide how you would like to perceive its length.

Certainly all of you have experienced an endless day and one that flies by in a moment.

It is all about the attention and definition you give it.

Decide to be the master of time rather than the victim of it.

It is a good exercise for all."

-VERONICA

133

World Energy

"We have shared before the importance of a good ebb and flow of energy in the linear reality. In this time frame of great transition to a higher level, it is important to maintain the consistency of a positive ebb and flow.

Much misalignment may occur when one becomes engaged in any way with the current negative energy that is being eliminated. It is very easy in your culture to participate with all the negativity even while not being in close physical proximity.

We realize all of you are interested in what is called the news of the day. However, the engagement of its energy improperly will only beg it to linger.

The advice of those spiritual may be effective to permanently eliminate such dramas eternally.

Consider keeping your own energy removed from these dramas as they dissipate. Refusing to enable the energy reinforces what is needed..... complete elimination.

We encourage all those in physical not to become distracted. The direct focus of your energy is imperative to the "clean up".

Imagine if you will, a very dirty room that must be cleaned.

The first several passes to eliminate the dirt always reveals the job to be much more difficult than thought. It is always important to focus upon the end result.... a clean room. Focusing on the dirt distracts one from the goal and can offer feelings of depression.

It is of a similar vein in your current surroundings. Remain clear about the end result.

Stay focused, rise above the fray. Keep your energy aligned until the new level is reached."

--VERONICA

134

Facing Difficulty

"Many times in the linear the energy becomes so thick and unbalanced, it becomes difficult to live through the moment. Events unfold from this vibration that are not the most desired ones.

What does one do when faced with such opposition to their well being?

It is important to keep one's thoughts clear from the "what ifs" that most likely have not manifested. If fear is allowed to run rampant within, the experience may turn into a much worse scenario than the first appearance.

Often one will embellish a poor situation by creating extra elements that were not in the original mix or the experience or lesson.

Keep yourself clear headed when going through a difficult moment. Realize that you were part of its creation, so the outcome is in your hands as well.

Think of the best possible result and stay fixed on that point. By allowing extra energy into it, there is risk of extending or continued creating of the difficulty.

Life is about experience. Not all of it is easy. At the end of the day it's how you rise to the adversity that results in your soul's evolution.

Keep focused.

Determine the lesson.

Stay within the parameters of that lesson.

Go with the flow of energy and allow the lesson to unfold. Keep in mind that it is an opportunity to evolve. There is no need for extra embellishment of the difficulty. Hold hands with your Soul and all will be well."

-VERONICA

135

Runaway Thoughts

"In the turbulent energy of the current time frame it is important to remember how important your thoughts are.

Many times when a probable negative situation arises, the thought process has the ability to run in various directions within the moment. Past experience can engage, raising the emotional levels to trigger a response that will render the difficulty into a reality.

All have participated in runaway thought. The initial presented moment a probability while within the mind, it will take flight allowing the thinker to mentally live through the event that has not occurred in the linear. This gives energy to the probability, often assisting in creating the event.

The mind is a powerful tool. Keeping thoughts on a positive pathway is not always easy. However, with practice one may discover that by not participating in a runaway thought, there is more opportunity to have more creative control over the physical experience.

Attempt to stay focused. Turn the corner to a more positive perspective. Curb the thought into what you would like the situation to be. It will be difficult but it is possible.

It is also important to understand how the physical body participates emotionally with runaway thoughts so that the body will feel the weariness of full engagements.

Stay calm. Allow your thoughts to create, however, reign in the panic driven runaway thoughts. It will make for a more productive participation.

You are what you think.

Think clearly.

Control fear.

Keep thoughts aligned with the soul.

It will help."

-VERONICA

136

Processing Fears

"In the linear life it can be extremely helpful to identify your true fears. Often a past moment projects upon a present moment, creating an environment of unhealthiness.

By taking an introspective moment with calmness, one is able to know exactly where the current fear originated.

Compounded fears (from multiple lives) are almost impossible to process and overcome. This is why core identification is so helpful.

All the lives that each of you participate in co-mingle to help create your current reality. Unresolved fears can reflect into the current situation making it fcel more complicated than it actually is.

When faced with the linear chaos that fear creates, it is important to remain clear about the fear.

Identify its origins; if the current life offers no explanation, proceed to investigation of past life moments.

The answer usually lies beneath the skin of a life that never had an opportunity to resolve the fear.

It is the not knowing or question mark in a current life that can find no logical explanation for the fear based participation that tends to create the imbalance.

It is a fact that all have had multiple experiences in the physical world. It would also stand to reason that the emotions and fears of those lives would remain intact with the individual's energy.

Attempt to bring your fears close to examine them. Often upon scrutiny they will lose their momentum to upset your current moment.

Know that your experience is vast and not limited to this life. Processing past fears can make this life better.

It is worth an investigation."

--VERONICA

137

Move Forward

It is important in the linear life not to let disappointment in events or people color your ability to create.

The expectations of the soul often are not prepared for the thick energy that the linear provides. Thus the intentions from the soul that wish to manifest, are sometimes difficult to bring through the physical environment.

Sensitive souls may become disillusioned by this process, sinking into forms of depression because of it.

We encourage all who have met with disappointment to move forward with all the gusto they can muster. A belief in your core values and abilities needs to come forward at all times. It is often not your energy that is the problem.

It is often the surrounding energy that is difficult to maneuver through.

Always be in touch with your center. Keep the dialogue of communication active from within.

If there is an opportunity to participate creatively, set aside the disappointment and try again.

The commitment to the endeavor may supersede all else.

Remember you are a spirit having a physical experience, not the other way around. Attach to your soulful energy and do not give up.

Do not allow disappointment to create your reality. Use your core energy to bypass the energy.

You can accomplish whatever it is you desire. Go for it with no reservations.

Believe in your energy and turn away from disappointment. Do not allow it to color your current perspective. Attempt a fresh approach. Leave it behind while moving forward in your reality."

-VERONICA

138

A Brave Soul
Embarks Upon The Journey

"The physical experience is a complicated one. Plans made in Spirit often go awry in the static energy of a world filled with unbalance.

A brave soul embarks upon the journey filled with hope and promise. The thickness of the environment distorts the intention leading many to wonder why they did this to begin with.

A swirl of negative energy blinds even the most evolved soul while navigating all the perils of this experience.

Many begin to endlessly circle the same experience, perhaps with different players. They know they are stagnant but cannot resolve a solution to change the inevitable outcome.

What should you do if you are stuck?

You are a physical representation of your soul. The God energy within is your most valuable asset.

A change of momentum or direction, no matter how small, will have effect on the energy flow. Your soul energy can redirect the moment.

Stop endlessly following the same pattern. Decide that the path you tread is no longer of value.

Reach towards the eternalness within. The noise of your reality is distracting. Turn down the chatter and go home to your soul within.

The soul, always available, will soothe and encourage more progress within. Eventually that internal moment will spill into your reality.

Becoming free flowing while physical is the best way to become "unstuck".

Focus on the soul and its flow. The rest will surely follow."

-VERONICA

139

Using Your Gifts

"Each soul as it becomes physical condenses the energy in order to come into the physical form. The abilities of spirit come forward often, sometimes a natural blend while other times as a surprise to the physical energy. All incarnate souls bring with them the sense of eternal knowledge. It depends upon the soul age and their physical awareness how much may manifest itself into linear participation.

We have spoken to many who ask for guidance in becoming more capable of participating with their gifts. In the current linear atmosphere it is imperative that all those who can should move into full participation.

Often it is self doubt that hinders the most. The comprehension that one is an eternal being having a physical experience often escapes the most advanced soul energy. It is important to realize that this God energy is in all of you. Attempting to dismiss it is often met by frustration as the physical tries to define what is missing.

Allow your self to embrace the eternal without definition. There is no need to be fearful or closed. The appropriate energy will come forward without worry.

It is time for the manifestation of the gifts within all of you. Allow them to come forward.

The eternal is rooted in a positive flow. More than enough energy to combat the negativity that exists in only the linear.

Tap into your soulful energy. You are able to make a difference. Bring your gifts forward and share them. It is time.

Leave the doubt behind and move forward to what is necessary both in the eternal and the linear.

You are gifted.

Use the gifts.

Make a difference."

-VERONICA

140

Owning Your True Potential

"Recognizing and owning one's true potential is often a difficult task in the linear life. A discovery often results when one truly lets go of the immediate dramas and becomes unified with their soulful selves.

The question surely raised is, "How does one do that?"

In the physical anyone can spin a drama into deeper and deeper moments. No one really needs assistance with that enactment. What one does need perspective on is the ability to lift up and out of drama.

Take always time to be with yourself. Spend quiet moments remembering who you are. Separate from the dramatics by providing a haven for yourself of harmony.

This translates into a walk, a restful moment, exercise, meditation, etc. Anything that draws your attention away from the thick energy.

If you are deeply entrenched it may take some time, so do not be discouraged with a lack of immediate results. It most likely took quite a bit of time to get where you are. So it will take time to work out of it.

There is no magic elixir in the linear to repair energy. It is a process that does take focus and determination.

Know that you are powerful enough to achieve the realignment. Most often it is the lack of confidence that keeps most apart from a resolution.

Close your eyes and feel your energy. If you are unclear take a small crystal in your hands that will enhance your ability to feel your electromagnetic energy. Allow yourself to feel it and become reacquainted with it.

It will be worth the effort.

Believe that it is possible.

Remember who you are.

All will be well."

-VERONICA

141

Hope

"Participating in the physical environment is extremely difficult. The most advanced souls often find themselves knee deep in the muck and mire of the dramatic linear. It has the potential to defeat the most powerful creative thoughts wistfully if one is not watchful.

While roaming through a life, the one sure tool available to all is hope. The belief that something is attainable is the strongest asset that anyone has. It is important to nurture and protect the ability. Physical life is much too hard to walk through without it.

No Matter what dramatic event unfolds, know that your ability to cherish a good outcome with anticipation is a critical ingredient in how it all plays out.

Do not be discouraged if at first glance it does not occur. Great focus is needed to keep hope alive and strong. A lot of you are simply out of practice, having given up a while back.

You have come here to learn great lessons, each of them unique unto you. Not all of them are easy, and actually that is by your design.

Maintain a good outlook, learn the lesson quickly with humility, all the while maintaining your relationship with hope.

We realize it is difficult. Nothing worth participating in ever is. You are a powerful energy. Do not lose sight of that. Keep the hope alive in you.

It is the best way."

-VERONICA

142

Those Who Incarnate With You

"Those who incarnate with you in life have a special place in the development of your soul. Not all participations are easy ones. Often a close energy will take on the role of antagonist to help you grow energetically through linear lessons.

The important thing is to realize that all that interact with you have value.

The levels of energy and focus may vary, but ultimately even the most negative one can bring forth much needed clarity.

The correct moment would be knowing when to dismiss a negative energy. Often they linger far too long in one's energy field. Knowing when the lesson is finished and moving on are indeed equally important.

The linear reality offers participation on many different levels. Just as often, extremely well matched energies participate with each other, bringing great joy.

It is important to maintain these energy connections as they can also give great energy support.

Move through life with your eyes wide open and your inner awareness intact.

Everyone you encounter does indeed have something to offer. Knowing how the exchanges work in your favor and against you is an opportunity to advance the soul.

Keep clear.

Keep calm.

Know when to continue, and...

Know when to stop and dismiss.

The linear offers much in this manner. You are here so participate. The advancement of your soul is in play."

-VERONICA

143

Paying Attention

"In the reality of your culture it is very easy to become an unconscious participant. It often begins when the energy becomes abrasive. The uncomfortable environments lead many to ignore the difficult energy because there is a belief that nothing can be accomplished anyway.

The lack of attention to one's own energy participation compounds the mass consciousness events even more. The result is an out of control reality that creates a continuous vicious circle.

Until one starts to pay attention to energy, especially their own, the cycle will continue to disintegrate the positive potential of each participant.

Your energy is a vital part of reality. Its participation creates the events in which you participate. To do it unconsciously you are essentially giving permission of creation to a random universe.

We would suggest taking notice of how you participate in your daily life. Do not leave creation to chance or others. Think clearly about yourself at all times. It is your reality as well as everyone else's.... you do get the opportunity for input. Be sure you are not sleep-walking when it presents itself.

Thought creates reality.

Be sure your awareness is in good shape so that you can create effectively.

Awaken yourself to who you are and the potential of creation you can bring to the table.

Wake up.

Become aware.

Feel the power of your thought and use it effectively.

Pay attention to your reality."

-VERONICA

Editor's note: Do not confuse VERONICA's use of the word "random" with the word "accident". They mean two completely different things. "Random" means unpredictable with certainty. The universe is this way in part because individual thoughts and choices are unpredictable with certainty.

144

Give Yourself a Chance

"Physical existence offers a great gift. As a new day dawns, a freshness occurs when the sun rises. The possibility of a new light against your cheek can help you create a new opportunity for evolution.

Do not forget the previous day no matter what the energy was. Positive or negative, it is a thread that weaves into the tapestry of your evolution. Be sure to include its texture as physical participation was meant to be a woven cloth of experience.

All the colors, textures, and weaves create the proper experience as one progresses through spiritual evolution. Attempt to view the whole piece of cloth when judging yourself on your progress. If one only focuses on one thread, it does not by any means define who you are as a whole.

Often one forgets this and becomes extremely judgmental in assessing the progress in the linear.

This judgment serves nothing and often disrupts and slows the evolution of your soul.

Decide that each day is a new thread with bountiful opportunity. Allow yourself to be bold when choosing the texture and color. If you were disappointed or unsatisfied with yesterday's weave, realize that it can all be changed this day.

Refresh.

Renew.

Give yourself a chance to change course. The self-judgment is unnecessary. It will only hinder the soul's progress.

Forgive.

Move Forward.

It is indeed a new day."

-VERONICA

145

Each Soul Chooses Its Path

"In times of difficulty many embark upon a pilgrimage to find an easement to their suffering. Depending upon the belief system, the true path to that relief is wrought with different steps. The end result, however, is always a reconnection to their spiritual cores.

One would suppose that more advanced souls would not have a problem with that, however, the path to evolution can become more complicated in that advancement.

All souls regardless of status, seek the clarity of a quiet threshold to create their reality eloquently.

It is important to quiet the noise of the linear while seeking the ability to create it: A true reality for those who are indeed participating in the linear.

Create if you will, a moment daily where the calmness of your thoughts supersedes all others.

Physical realities are filled with activity and drama. Each soul chooses its path through that noise of participation. Stepping away from the noise is essential for clear creativity.

If you are embedded in complicated drama, decide to step away until a moment of clarity is attained.

The soul is supreme in its ability to navigate the path to your evolution. Allow it a quiet moment to do its job. The soul desperately moves towards advancement. In a moment of silence, allow it to do so.

If the soul is not distracted it will lead you to ultimate advancement.

Simply silence the noise.

The soul will do the rest.

Allow it.

It is possible."

-VERONICA

146

Now

"This day is the representation of your "now". To spend this moment lamenting the past and worrying about the future does not allow you to participate in the creative abilities of your soul energy.

To create the perfect now, it is important as we've said, to go inward to the soul to find clarity. It is also an important part of the linear experience to go outward as well. It can be achieved with more forcefulness in conjunction with the inward journey.

The ebb and flow of energy which is a vital part of all creation can exist between the inward and the outward. For some it can be the ultimate experience.

To achieve the outward one must participate fully in the physical condition. Attempt to create and recreate your linear reality with integrity and colorfulness. For the moment, maintain your present. Compliment it with the inward journey while remembering to create a reality outwardly.

The two ideas are separate.

Physical reality was meant to be an expression of your soul. Learn the lessons yes, however, appreciate it for whatever it is. It is your opportunity to be totally present in your 'now'."

-VERONICA

147

Energy Healing

"As the soul inhabits the body it can become proficient at reassembling the structure and function of the biological form.

There are those of you who possess the ability to harness their own energy in assisting others in this process. Some have accepted the calling while others remain unsure. It is most important to investigate the stirrings of healing abilities that emanate from your soul. Most of you are ancient healers that have chosen to return to the physical in this time frame. To ignore the whispers of your abilities is indeed tragic.

Thousands of years ago in your reality, the well-being of the biological form was maintained through energetic means. Some of you were participating in that time and have memory of it being so.

The inter-connection energetically between healers creates a grid of strength that combined, can reassemble biology in a profound way. We beseech all to listen intently to these memories.

It is a grand time of consciousness raising. The biological forms will need support and healing through the transformation.

If you are experiencing the impulses of energy please pay attention. The magnificence of the soul comes forward because it is needed.

It is why you are here."

-VERONICA

148

You Are Valuable

"Often in the physical, the value of the incarnation is dismissed by the linear person involved. It is imperative to understand that you as an energy having a human life is valuable to the soul.

The physical is not a smooth environment. It is easy to become over involved with the dramas, forgetting the relationship with one's own soul. Poor choices, difficult times, and inadequate participation can contribute to the low esteem that many have for their current incarnation.

Realize that no matter what the circumstance, your soul will seek the value of the experience. Of course it is better to be clear, but even the most distorted difficult experience creates opportunity for the soul to evolve.

The most dire events can create the most growth. Your soul appreciates and values those moments no matter what they are.

We encourage you to accept this appreciation, thus creating a healthy ebb and flow of energy.

You are valuable to your soul. Each day that you participate in the linear presents a new opportunity for its growth.

Attempt to find the clarity to think through each day. Create the ebb and flow energy that will make the journey more comfortable.

Know your worth.

Your soul does."

-VERONICA

149

Action vs. Reaction

"The reality of the earth plane at this time is chaotic at best. Most are attempting to regain their balance upon very slippery paths. It is always so when the consciousness of an environment is expanding and raising its vibration.

It is important at such times to maintain one's perspective in a positive way. Upheaval and negativity can present themselves, so it is up to the individual soul to choose its path during these times.

If one merely reacts to whatever is presented through the mass consciousness, then individual focus power can be compromised. It is always preferred to be proactive while moving through the dramas. This way, one is able to introduce one's energy to the situation purely so that their positive influence may help remedy the creation of the reality.

In essence, it is better to remain individualistic in any situation. Inserting one's energy that is active is important.

If one allows a reaction to occur then the blend of energy creating the situation is compromised.

Stay focused and active while participating in your day. If something does occur, process the moment without reaction, then continue your creative flow. It will help with the co-creation.

Be an energy of action.

Allow your soul to flow through with power into the reality.

It has the potential to change the moment.

Ready, set, action.

Try it."

-VERONICA

150

Dismiss The Trivia

"When one decides to embark upon a physical incarnation, it is from a place of peace and clarity. The denseness of the linear that unfolds often tends to confuse and depress souls that are seeking evolution.

The younger souls complain, "This is just too hard.", while the older souls lament, "Why did I come here?"

There is a great deal of pressure put upon those who strive to live a life void of difficulty. It seems from every corner another debacle rears its head even before the previous one has resolved itself. Most are weary of the fight. Most begin to feel victim of an unfriendly universe. The real tragedy is that most begin to doubt their own creative abilities due to what is around them. The focus upon creating opportunity to evolve is compromised by the loss of confidence.

When faced with all the diversity, one must remain steadfast. Remind yourself of what you are capable of by remaining focused on the goal.

Stirring up your energy is often a good remedy. By doing so, one can often become reacquainted with a key ingredient within that which was lost in the shuffle before.

Do not let opinions of others deter you from success. You all live in a culture that is full of opinions. It does not mean they are factual or strong enough to affect your path.

Remain focused.

Dismiss the trivia.

Be confident. Make it your business to know yourself. Acknowledge your abilities.

No opinion can change who you are at a core level.

You are capable."

-VERONICA

151

Mistakes

"In times of trouble, the world around the self feels like it is crumbling. A feeling of powerlessness can envelop even the most evolved energies.

One may feel responsible for choices that can be perceived as mistakes. Know that choices are what physical reality is all about. A choice that may feel right and ends up creating negative energy is often regarded as a mistake. The self can become depressed over that choice and become fearful of making future choices. Thus a feeling of judgment, while feeling stuck begins to permeate the reality. When this occurs, fear and depression end up taking over the process by which the soul creates its life in the physical.

How to remedy this is the next question.

Know that every perceived mistake can deliver a lesson that can change your life for the better. It is important to own the mistake, observe its energy, and find the lesson within. To do that one must remain non-judgmental of the self. It is difficult to do, but with practice and most importantly patience, it can be achieved.

Every physical experience can be a tool to grow and prosper. Keeping the judgment out of one's daily activities is a good start.

Self-judgment is the most difficult of issues to overcome. It is usually a life long process, but along the way, if handled with clarity minus anger, it can be achieved."

-VERONICA

152

Spiritual Survival In The Linear

"Deciding to participate in physical life is a complicated choice as one becomes more evolved as an energy. In the early moments, younger souls often blindly leap from one life to the other simply attempting to understand the process. When some clarity is finally achieved, the life patterns are somewhat confused.

It is important in your "now moment" to pay attention to the feelings of your soul. To survive in any physical culture, one needs to understand the spiritual survival needs, as well as the physical ones.

Playing out dramas is often considered a good way to achieve understanding in lessons. One should be aware that becoming the drama is not the best participation. All of you have felt overwhelmed in a drama out of control.

That is because those who participate do not trust the inner soulful indicators or indicators of which should be enacted next.

By ignoring the soul, one can flounder aimlessly in the linear and its dramas.

Stop often. Listen. Feel what some may refer to as your gut. It is actually your soul's barometer giving you the correct guidance needed to survive and thrive through daily dramas and lessons.

If you feel nothing, then it is time to re-acquaint yourself. Waste not time proceeding to the arena of your soul. Whatever the method, get there.

Stop the dramatic presentation. It's most likely a circular pattern with no conclusion in sight.

To soulfully survive the linear, one must walk away from dramatics that are out of control. The need for victory in them is an illusion of the physical.

Return to who you are. Find comfort in the silence. It is not a defeat to do so. It is actually a victory."

-VERONICA

153

In Regard To Relationships

"In regard to relationships with others, the image of the self plays a huge role in how they are played out in the linear.

It is very difficult to love another if one does not love themselves.

We are not speaking of a physical attraction, which is often labeled as love. We are speaking of the deep connection that has roots in the unconditional.

A good look at how you participate in your own energy will help you in how you love others in a relationship.

Start by being aware of your own energy. How often do you feel in harmony with yourself? If you are at odds in a relationship, more than likely you are finding difficulty in your own energy.

Everything in the reality you participate in is based on an ebb and flow of energy. This is true right down to the molecules that create the solid moments.

By taking care of your energy you enable yourself to attract energies that match your own.

So, if you are only participating halfway with your own energy, you are going to attract someone who is half of what you really want.

Tend to the garden that is yours. By doing so you create through the ebb and flow someone who is worthy of participating with you.

If you are already in a relationship, keeping your energy balanced will help bring clarity to the union. You may find they are not so attractive after all.

Being honest with the self and nurturing your relationships with your self will bring forward the perfect opportunity.

Consider the love of self. It may remedy all the difficulty."

-VERONICA

154

The Next Step

"Many have spoken of going internally to the soul. It is indeed a good exercise that we have spoken of many times. However, the return to the soul is appropriate in many ways, but once reuniting, there is another important step.

Having a physical experience is important for the soul's evolution. The participation leads to greater understanding for the complete energy to grow. Often while participating in the linear, the focus becomes so intense that the soulful energy becomes cut off from its core. Thus the advice of many linear practices to return to the soul.

Once returned, what does one accomplish? Does it alleviate all the turmoil that the dramatics of physical involvement brings?

Most likely not in the early moments. However, once reconnected, the soul having the linear experience may be able to bring the soulful energy into their physical more abundantly, thus alleviating any suffering that may be occurring.

Practice feeling what the soul says.

You have already silenced much of the linear drama to get to the core of your soul. Now join with that energy while making choices in your physical linear life. Listen to the voice of your soul rather than the chatter of those who occupy space in your current physical environment.

Most of those energies are processing their own abilities to evolve and may be of no assistance in your development.

Attempt to listen only to the sounds of your own energy. That way you are acting instead of reacting while on your path of evolution: Much better to be in charge than a follower.

Eventually all followers will be leaders if they allow this process to occur. God, Yahweh, Buddha, Christ, Source Energy... all favor the empowered moment rather than the follower moment.

All of source wishes to become mobile in whatever level of environment it currently resides. This is a natural process of energy. There is nothing to fear, only the self-constructed facades that linger in your own mind.

Connect, blend, and reestablish yourself as a soul while still being physical. Let your energy in. Participate.

It is the next step."

-VERONICA

155

The Results May Amaze You

"In the current moment of this particular time-frame, it is most easy to step into despairing thoughts. Reality has a way of coming after your well-being when it is allowed to run rampant without control.

In bad times it is important to retain the validity of your own thoughts. Clearly, the impact of others participating in negative processes can lead the most powerful energies to slip upon the slope of the mountain they wish to climb.

Linear reality is based upon a give and take of energy. Being clear with your own thoughts is somewhat easier than exchanging thoughts and energies with others.
It is important to be completely comfortable with your energy. This will lead to a better creation during co-creating and mass consciousness creations.

Do not allow others to diminish what you know to be your truth within yourself. Stand strong with what you know is a product of your own energy.

Giving and taking the essence of that energy is what the physical experience is all about for you. It is your journey. Your particular energy pattern is contributing to the mass consciousness of the complete reality... and it does make a difference.

Remembering who you are should be followed by being who you are in physical reality.

It is possible.

The results of "being who you are" in this reality may amaze you."

-VERONICA

156

Emotions Are A Wild Card To Many

"An important part of physical existence is participating with one's own feelings or emotions. A balance between thought and emotion is essential in the creative process.

Emotions are a wild card to many. One often feels that by even participating in a small part of their feelings they are opening themselves up to a whole world of uncertainty. By far most have a better understanding of their thoughts than their feelings.

It is important to investigate the emotions to see what the trigger is. Often a reluctance to do so comes from a negative past experience, not necessarily from the current life.

Physical participation offers great opportunity to evolve. The whole package does include emotion. Whenever possible extend yourself out of your comfort zone. Explore the ranges of emotion within. It is actually a sign of great strength to boldly move into an emotional moment. We realize that some cultures state otherwise, however, true advancement is only achieved through thought and emotion.

Let yourself examine the probabilities.

You can control how much in your own sense of comfortable timing.

Without allowing your thoughts to mingle in your feelings, the process of evolution will take longer.

Give it a try. Your feelings are unique unto you.

Full participation will result in a recipe of your evolvement."

-VERONICA

APPENDIX

(VERONICA's Forward Message From Volume II)

Many writings have been shared during the path of "Inner Whispers". All of them... through the gracious hand of April who allows us, VERONICA, to speak.

Our intention is to reach out to those who feel sharply, the isolation of physical. Spirit is more accustomed to the blend, which most of you seek throughout your incarnation.

We understand the process.

Never feel alone for we are always focused on the souls of those who need assistance. It is our intention to enlighten and to share a perspective to help you on your journey home. We have great affection for your soul.

The longevity of our relationship supersedes the writing of this book.

Though without physical form, we are not without heart & compassion for those evolving their way through the physical experience. 'Tis the reason for our participation... no other.

Feel our presence and be comforted. We are indeed real, our consciousness ever expanding towards evolution. Our hope is that you will journey with us to the eternal. We are merely participating at a different frequency and sometimes it provides a clearer view.

We are your constant supporter with true belief in the power of your soul.

Your friend,

VERONICA

About the Author

April Crawford is an AMAZON Top 50 Best Selling Author, and, April is also one of the world's most naturally talented and adept Full Body Open Deep Trance Channels and Spiritual Mediums.   April and the Entity/Guide VERONICA have consulting clients in most countries of the world.

April's spiritual newsletter, *"Inner Whispers"*, is written by highly evolved nonphysical entities and guides, primarily by VERONICA, and is read by tens of thousands of readers each week. It is available (free) at www.InnerWhispers.net

About The Author

April currently lives in Los Angeles, California with her husband, Allen, and her many pets.***

OTHER BOOKS
BY
APRIL CRAWFORD

"Inner Whispers": Messages From A Spirit Guide (Volume I)

Available also for Kindle and Nook

For more information: www.InnerWhispersTheBook.com

"Inner Whispers": Messages From A Spirit Guide (Volume II)

Available also for Kindle and Nook

For more information: www.InnerWhispersBookTwo.com

"Parting Notes": A Connection With The Afterlife

Available also for Kindle and Nook

For more information: www.PartingNotes.com

Other Books by April Crawford

"In The AfterLife":
A Chronicle Of Our Experiences On The Other Side
Available also for Kindle and Nook

Ashram Tang… a Story… and a Discovery
Available also for Kindle and Nook
www.AshramTang.com

Reflections of a Spiritual Astronaut: Book I
Available for Kindle and Nook

Reflections of a Spiritual Astronaut: Book II
Available for Kindle and Nook

your life and its choices: THE RECIPE FOR ASCENTION TO ANOTHER PLANE "A" TO "Z"
By Ish and Osco (Spirit Guides) via April Crawford
Available for Kindle and Nook

Deep Trance Channeling Sessions:
Special Edition No. 1
Available for Kindle and Nook

Other Books by April Crawford

For more information about the Author or about True Open Deep Trance Channeling: www.AprilCrawford.com

For the free spiritual newsletter *"Inner Whispers"* www.InnerWhispers.net

For personal telephone or in-person consultations via April Crawford, Personal Appearances, or Media Interviews contact Allen at AprilReadings@aol.com

***

Made in the USA
San Bernardino, CA
03 June 2014